THE ULTIMATE
TENNESSEE TITANS
TRIVIA BOOK

A Collection of Amazing Trivia Quizzes and Fun Facts for Die-Hard Titans Fans!

Ray Walker

Exclusive Free Book

Crazy Sports Stories

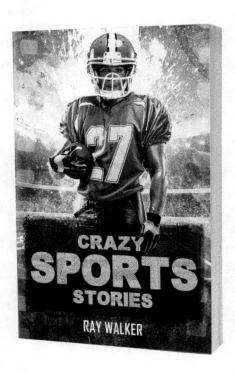

As a thank you for getting a copy of this book I would like to offer you a free copy of my book Crazy Sports Stories which comes packed with interesting stories from your favorite sports such as Football, Hockey, Baseball, Basketball and more.

Grab your free copy over at

RayWalkerMedia.com/Bonus

CONTENTS

INTRODUCTION

Team fandom should be inspirational. Our attachment to our favorite team should fill us with pride, excitement, loyalty, and a sense of fulfillment in knowing that we are part of a community with many other fans who feel the same way.

Titan fans are no exception. With a rich, successful history in the NFL, the Tennessee Titans have inspired their supporters to strive for greatness with their tradition of colorful players, memorable eras, big moves, and unique moments.

This book is meant to be a celebration of those moments and an examination of a collection of interesting, impressive, and important details that allow us to understand the full stories behind the players and the team.

You may use the book as you wish. Each chapter contains 20 quiz questions in a mixture of multiple-choice and true-or-false formats, an answer key (don't worry, it's on a separate page!), and a section of 10 "Did You Know" facts about the team.

Some will use it to test themselves with the quiz questions. How much Titan history did you really know? How many of the finer points can you remember? Some will use it competitively (isn't

1

that the heart of sports?), waging contests with friends and fellow devotees to see who can lay claim to being the biggest fan. Some will enjoy it as a learning experience, gaining insight to enrich their fandom and add color to their understanding of their favorite team. Still others may use it to teach, sharing the wonderful anecdotes inside to inspire a new generation of fans to hop aboard the Titan bandwagon.

Whatever your purpose may be, we hope you enjoy delving into the amazing background of Titan football!

For the record, information and statistics in this book are current up to the beginning of 2021. The Titans will surely topple more records and win more awards as the seasons pass, so keep this in mind when you're watching the next game with your friends, and someone starts a conversation with "Did you know…"

CHAPTER 1:

ORIGINS & HISTORY

QUIZ TIME!

1. In which year did the Oiler/Titan franchise begin playing?

   a. 1960

   b. 1965

   c. 1970

   d. 1975

2. The franchise was nearly called the Tennessee Hot Wings, partly to reflect the team's southern culture (Nashville chicken in particular) and partly to honor a defunct rugby team from the city by that name.

   a. True

   b. False

3. How was the nickname "Titans" chosen for the team?

   a. It was chosen as something that would theoretically compare favorably in battle with other semi-mythical NFL nicknames, like Giants and Vikings.

b. The team owner also owned many businesses in the metal industry under the name "Titan Steel Holdings" and wanted to create synergy with the team.

c. The team owner wanted a name with heroic qualities and thought "Titans" would reflect the numerous Greek aspects of the city of Nashville.

d. It was a throwback to a professional baseball team that had played in Nashville during the 1950s and 60s.

4. In which season did the Titans begin to play in Nissan Stadium?

   a. 1996
   b. 1997
   c. 1998
   d. 1999

5. Who was the founder of the Tennessee Titans?

   a. Susie Adams Strunk
   b. Thomas S. Smith
   c. Bud Adams
   d. Tom Landry

6. Which of the following has never been an actual name for the franchise?

   a. Tennessee Titans
   b. Houston Titans
   c. Houston Oilers
   d. Tennessee Oilers

7. The Tennessee Titans won more games than any other AFC team during the period between 1990-1999.

    a. True
    b. False

8. How many times have the Titans won a division title?

    a. 10 times: 4 in the AFL and 6 in the NFL
    b. 13 times: 6 in the AFL and 7 in the NFL
    c. 15 times: 6 in the AFL and 9 in the NFL
    d. 18 times: 8 in the AFL and 10 in the NFL

9. How long was the Titans' longest playoff drought?

    a. Eight years, from 1970 through 1977, after the team joined the NFL
    b. Eight years, from 2009 through 2016, when the team cycled through four different head coaches
    c. Eleven years, from 2002 through 2012, when the NFL expanded and the Titans moved from the AFC Central to the AFC South Division
    d. A and B are tied for the longest drought

10. Where do the Tennessee Titans rank among NFL franchises in Super Bowl championships won?

    a. Tied for 5th all-time in the NFL
    b. 8th all-time in the NFL
    c. 14th all-time in the NFL
    d. Tied for last all-time in the NFL

11. How did the Titans fare during their 20th anniversary season after moving to Tennessee?

a. Missed the playoffs

b. Lost in the divisional round to the Baltimore Ravens

c. Lost in the AFC Championship game to the Kansas City Chiefs

d. Lost in the Super Bowl to the St. Louis Rams

12. The first Titan ever to be named as the franchise's representative as a member of the NFL All-Pro First Team was safety Ken Houston, who played for the team in Houston in 1971.

a. True

b. False

13. After the AFL/NFL merger in 1970, which team did the Houston Oilers face in their first NFL game (which resulted in a 19-7 victory)?

a. Miami Dolphins

b. Cincinnati Bengals

c. Cleveland Browns

d. Pittsburgh Steelers

14. What were the details surrounding the Titans' first shutout in the NFL?

a. It was a win in 1970, 10-0, over the Cleveland Browns.

b. It was a loss in 1970, 7-0, to the Dallas Cowboys.

c. It was a loss in 1970, 44-0, to the St. Louis Cardinals.

d. It was a win in 1972, 21-0, over the Buffalo Bills.

15. Who kicked the first field goal for the franchise?

a. Billy Cannon

b. Steve Johnson

c. George Blanda

d. Bruce Maher

16. As of 2021, Tennessee is tied with the Pittsburgh Steelers and Green Bay Packers as the franchises that have sent the most players to the Pro Bowl.

a. True

b. False

17. How did Tennessee fare in its first-ever playoff run after joining the NFL?

a. Lost in the wild card playoffs to the Denver Broncos

b. Beat the Denver Broncos, then lost in the divisional playoffs to the New England Patriots

c. Beat the Denver Broncos and San Diego Chargers, then lost in the AFC Championship to the Pittsburgh Steelers

d. Beat the Miami Dolphins and New England Patriots, then lost in the AFC Championship to the Pittsburgh Steelers

18. What is Houston's franchise record for most victories recorded by the club in a single AFL regular season (which were 14 games long)?

a. 9 wins

b. 11 wins

c. 12 wins

d. 14 wins

19. What is the name of the Titans' mascot?

a. Hercules the Titan, chosen as a symbol of strength from many Greek God options

b. Gruff the Grizzly, chosen as the most ferocious of all bears indigenous to Tennessee

c. T-Rac the Raccoon, chosen because the raccoon is Tennessee's official state animal

d. Turbo the Gladiator, chosen because the franchise wanted the mascot to stand for size, speed, and strength

20. During their time in the AFL, the Houston Oilers actually competed against a team named the Titans. For the first three years, the Oilers shared a division with the New York Titans and Houston had a 6 – 0 record against that club.

a. True
b. False

QUIZ ANSWERS

1. A – 1960

2. B – False

3. C – The team owner wanted a name with heroic qualities and thought "Titans" would reflect the numerous Greek aspects of the city of Nashville.

4. D – 1999

5. C – Bud Adams

6. B – Houston Titans

7. B – False

8. A – 10 times, 4 in the AFL and 6 in the NFL

9. D –A and B are tied for the longest drought

10. D – Tied for last all-time in the NFL

11. A – Missed the playoffs

12. A – True

13. D – Pittsburgh Steelers

14. C – It was a loss in 1970, 44 – 0, to the St. Louis Cardinals.

15. C – George Blanda

16. B – False

17. D – Beat the Miami Dolphins and New England Patriots, then lost in the AFC Championship to the Pittsburgh Steelers

18. B – 11 wins

19. C – T-Rac the raccoon, chosen because the raccoon is Tennessee's official state animal

20. A – True

DID YOU KNOW?

1. The franchise has averaged one stadium per decade during its existence in the AFL and NFL. As the Houston Oilers, the team spent time in Jeppesen Stadium at the University of Houston, Rice Stadium at Rice University, and the Houston Astrodome. In Tennessee, they followed the same pattern, playing first at Liberty Bowl Memorial Stadium at the University of Memphis and then Vanderbilt Stadium at Vanderbilt University, before settling into their own Nissan Stadium.

2. Tennessee's worst won-loss record ever was a dismal 1 – 13. As the Houston Oilers, the club actually sank this low in back-to-back seasons in 1972 and 1973 before climbing back to .500 the following year.

3. Nissan Stadium, the current home of the Titans, is located in Nashville and has undergone three name changes since its inception. It began its existence as Adelphia Coliseum in 1999, which was shortened to the Coliseum in 2002. It became LP Field in 2006 and took on the Nissan name in 2015.

4. While the Titans are an anchor tenant of Nissan Stadium, it is not their home exclusively. The Tennessee State University Tigers play there, as do the Nashville FC of Major League Soccer. It is also a common venue for musical acts or international soccer matches.

5. As a new team entering the AFL in 1960, the Houston Oilers paid a $25,000 franchise fee for the right to join the league. For context, when the Houston Texans joined the NFL in 2002, they paid an expansion fee of $700 million.

6. The first touchdown in franchise history was a long one. In its inaugural game in the AFL, Houston Oiler quarterback George Blanda found wide receiver Charlie Hennigan open for a 43-yard score, giving Houston the lead in an eventual 37-22 victory over the Oakland Raiders.

7. Tennessee's biggest NFL rival is debated but is generally thought to be the Indianapolis Colts because the two teams are in the same division and have often battled for success in the league. The Colts have a major advantage in the head-to-head rivalry, with 35 wins to the Titans' 17, but in their one playoff meeting, after the 1999 season, the Titans came out on top with a 19-16 victory.

8. Tennessee's franchise record for most victories in a single regular season is 13, which they have reached three times in history. They hit this pinnacle twice consecutively in 1999 and 2000 and they tied the mark in 2008.

9. When the franchise was still the Houston Oilers, in 1975, a cheerleading squad was established and name the Derrick Dolls. They have continued to support the team ever since but took on the more politically correct name Tennessee Titans Cheerleaders when the team moved to Nashville and switched nicknames in 1999.

10. In the beginning, the Houston Oilers started as well as a franchise could, winning back-to-back AFL championships during their first two seasons of existence in 1960 and 1961. They even made it to a third straight championship game in 1962 but lost in double overtime to the Dallas Texans.

CHAPTER 2:

JERSEYS & NUMBERS

QUIZ TIME!

1. When they began playing in the AFL in 1960, the Houston Oilers used what color scheme for their home and away uniforms?

    a. Midnight black, silver, and white
    b. Forest green, brown, and white
    c. Columbia blue, scarlet red, and white
    d. Columbia blue, rusty orange, and white

2. The Nos. 0 and 00 have been banned from circulation by Tennessee's ownership, as they are seen to represent a losing attitude.

    a. True
    b. False

3. During how many seasons in the history of the Houston Oiler/Tennessee Titan franchise has the team worn a red jersey?

    a. 0
    b. 1

c. 6

d. 10

4. Two excellent Tennessee pass-catchers each wore No. 89 with the team. Who were these two skilled players?

   a. Wide receiver Nate Washington and tight end Jared Cook

   b. Wide receivers Kevin Dyson and Haywood Jeffires

   c. Tight ends Delanie Walker and Jonnu Smith

   d. Wide receiver Webster Slaughter and tight end Frank Wychek

5. In which year was approval given for player names to appear on the backs of Houston Oiler jerseys?

   a. 1960

   b. 1965

   c. 1970

   d. 1973

6. Which jersey number proved to be the best seller with Titan fans in 2018, the year they introduced popular new uniforms?

   a. Quarterback Marcus Mariota's No. 8

   b. Running back Derrick Henry's No. 22

   c. Defensive tackle Jurrell Casey's No. 99

   d. Cornerback Malcolm Butler's No. 21

7. The white jerseys worn by Tennessee are often said to have been "jinxed" and therefore the team avoids wearing them during the Super Bowl whenever the choice is theirs.

a. True

b. False

8. During the 1984 NFL season, the Houston Oilers wore a patch on their shoulder to commemorate what?

  a. The passing of the team's first quarterback, the legendary George Blanda

  b. The 10th anniversary of the team's AFL championship victory

  c. The 25th anniversary of the team's inception

  d. The first Super Bowl to be held in Houston, at the Astrodome

9. Over the years, the Titan uniform has included multiple shades of blue. Which of the following shades has NOT been included in the color scheme?

  a. Royal blue

  b. Columbia blue

  c. Navy blue

  d. Titans blue

10. Running back Dickie Post wore it for two starts in 1971. Kicker Skip Butler wore it from 1972 to 1977. Then, almost three decades passed before kicker Rob Bironas finally wore it in 2005 for Tennessee. Which number was it?

  a. No. 2

  b. No. 11

  c. No. 28

  d. No. 39

11. Twenty-three players have worn No. 33 for the Titans. Which of these players scored the most career touchdowns?

    a. Running back Dion Lewis
    b. Wide receiver Ronnie Harmon
    c. Running back Mike Rozier
    d. Running back Gary Brown

12. Star quarterback Steve McNair is the only Titan ever to have worn the No. 9 on his jersey and will continue to be the only one as his number is now retired.

    a. True
    b. False

13. Franchise icon Eddie George was so attached to No. 27 while playing running back for Tennessee that he used it in all of the following ways afterward, except for which one?

    a. Making sure that his custom-built home was placed in a location where he could have the street address be No. 27
    b. As his entrant number while running a half marathon for charity
    c. Incorporated into the signature of his autograph
    d. In the title of a bar and grill he owns in Ohio

14. How many jersey numbers have the Tennessee Titans retired for their former players?

    a. 3
    b. 5

c. 8

d. 11

15. Which player competed for the Oilers/Titans for just seven seasons, the shortest tenure of anyone whose number has been retired by the franchise?

a. Quarterback Warren Moon

b. Defensive end Elvin Bethea

c. Defensive back Jim Norton

d. Running back Earl Campbell

16. Eight players have worn the No. 1 for Tennessee, and every single one of them was a quarterback.

a. True

b. False

17. Lucky No. 7 has been worn by 11 Tennessee players over the years. Which athlete wore it for the longest time?

a. Quarterback Dan Pastorini

b. Punter Reggie Roby

c. Quarterback Billy Volek

d. Kicker Tony Zendejas

18. In their most recent jersey retirement, the Titans decided to honor two players at the same time. Whose numbers did they retire together?

a. Guard Mike Munchak and offensive tackle Bruce Matthews

b. Quarterback Warren Moon and running back Earl Campbell

    c. Quarterback Steve McNair and running back Eddie George

    d. Linebackers Brian Orakpo and Wesley Woodyard

19. Which number did star quarterback Ryan Tannehill, who was named the NFL's Comeback Player of the Year in 2019, wear?

    a. No. 5

    b. No. 8

    c. No. 11

    d. No. 17

20. The Titans have retired more jersey numbers than any other NFL franchise has.

    a. True

    b. False

QUIZ ANSWERS

1. C – Columbia blue, scarlet red, and white

2. B – False

3. B – 1

4. D – Wide receiver Webster Slaughter and tight end Frank Wychek

5. A – 1960

6. A – Quarterback Marcus Mariota's No. 8

7. B – False

8. C – The 25th anniversary of the team's inception

9. A – Royal blue

10. A – No. 2

11. C – Running back Mike Rozier

12. B – False

13. A – Making sure that his custom-built home was placed in a location where he could have the street address be No. 27

14. C – 8

15. D – Running back Earl Campbell

16. B – False

17. A – Quarterback Dan Pastorini

18. C – Quarterback Steve McNair and running back Eddie George

19. D – No. 17

20. B – False

DID YOU KNOW?

1. The Tennessee Titan logo features a trio of red stars surrounding the letter "T." The three stars are a nod to the Tennessee State Flag, on which they represent the different regions of the state.

2. The highest number ever sported by a Titan is No. 99. Defensive tackle Jurrell Casey put his stamp on this, holding the number from 2011 to 2018 before fellow defensive lineman Jadeveon Clowney took it over in 2020.

3. Titan wide receiver Corey Davis initially thought his jersey number was a prank. When attending Western Michigan University, the team gave him No. 84, which was the same number Davis' older brother wore while playing for archrival Central Michigan University. Davis kept the number anyway and had success with it, bringing it into the NFL with him when he was drafted by Tennessee.

4. After franchise legend Warren Moon left the Oilers in 1993, his No. 1 was kept out of circulation. Oddly, after Moon retired in 2000, Tennessee allowed kicker Gary Anderson to wear the number for two seasons before retiring it for good in Moon's honor in 2006.

5. For a two-year period when the team had moved to Tennessee but was still known as the Oilers, players wore an alternate logo that featured combined elements of their

traditional oil derrick with those of the Tennessee state flag. This ended in 1999 when the team became known as the Titans.

6. Houston Oiler owner Bud Adams grabbed the rights to the use of the Columbia blue color upon the founding of the AFL. Both Adams and Kansas City Chiefs founder Lamar Hunt initially wanted to use Columbia blue as their franchise's main color but Adams beat Hunt to the punch, leaving Hunt to go with his second choice instead and creating the color schemes that Titan and Chief fans know today.

7. Superstition may have scared some Titans away from wearing the No. 13. Only three players in franchise history have worn the number in a game for the franchise and only wide receiver Kendall Wright kept it for more than two seasons.

8. Since 1973, the NFL no longer allows players to wear jersey No. 0 or 00. No Titan or Oiler ever wore No. 0 in the 14 seasons before this change, so it will never be used in franchise history. Interestingly, kicker Ken Burrough wore No. 00 before the rule change and was allowed to keep it until his retirement in 1981, making him the last NFL player to sport the digits.

9. The highest number ever retired by the Tennessee Titans is No. 74, belonging to offensive lineman Bruce Matthews. Matthews lasted an incredible 19 seasons with the franchise in a physically demanding position, retiring in 2001 at age 40.

10. The original logo used by the franchise was an oil rig derrick, which was featured prominently on the team's helmets and was known as "Ol' Riggy."

CHAPTER 3:

CATCHY NICKNAMES

QUIZ TIME!

1. The 1992 Houston Oilers were the first team to be called "The Greatest Show On Turf," a nickname that was later stolen by what other team's record-setting offense?

    a. New England Patriots
    b. Atlanta Falcons
    c. St. Louis Rams
    d. San Francisco 49ers

2. Titan running back Eddie George was often referred to as "Smooth Eddie" thanks not to his elusive running style but to his signature shaved head.

    a. True
    b. False

3. The long-time home of the Oilers, the Houston Astrodome, was also commonly known by which popular nickname?

    a. "The Miracle Palace"
    b. "The Texas Bubble"

c. "Football Heaven"

d. "The Eighth Wonder of the World"

4. Which Tennessee player was affectionately known by players and fans as "the Freak" due to his speed, wingspan, and vertical leap?

    a. Quarterback Steve McNair

    b. Running back Eddie George

    c. Defensive end Jevon Kearse

    d. Wide receiver Kevin Dyson

5. Why was Houston Oiler wide receiver Billy Johnson known around the league as "White Shoes"?

    a. During a punt return for a touchdown in college, Johnson's shoes flew off as he was running, leaving him in just his socks, making it look as though he was wearing white shoes.

    b. In high school, he accepted a dare to dye his shoes differently from the black color worn by the rest of the team.

    c. Johnson was considered to excel in games played during nice weather (where his shoes would stay clean) but, when it was snowy or muddy, he would be easily shut down.

    d. Whenever Johnson went out on the town for a night of dinner and dancing, he would wear his best black suit and immaculately polished white shoes.

6. Which of the following is not a nickname that has been applied to Titan running back Derrick Henry?

a. "The Steamroller"

b. "King Henry"

c. "The Little Tractor"

d. "Shocka"

7. Tennessee quarterback Ryan Fitzpatrick was known as "The Amish Rifle" because of his bushy, overgrown beard and strong throwing arm.

a. True

b. False

8. Which unflattering nickname was Oiler quarterback Chris Chandler given due to his tendency to suffer injuries?

a. "Training Room"

b. "5 Start"

c. "Crystal Chandelier"

d. "Fragile Contents"

9. Why was Tennessee cornerback Adam Jones better known as "Pacman" throughout his NFL career?

a. Because he gobbled up passes thrown by opposing quarterbacks

b. Because he changed directions often and on a dime, just like the popular video game character

c. Because he claimed that playing video games kept his hand-eye coordination sharp for football

d. Because he played his college football in the Pac-10 conference

10. Titan franchise quarterback Steve McNair went by which one-word nickname?

a. "Champ"

b. "Padre"

c. "Sir"

d. "Air"

11. Which Oiler player was known to fans and teammates by the nickname "Ghost," thanks to a popular movie with a connection to his name?

a. Center Chuck Thomas

b. Defensive tackle Mike Golic

c. Tight end Dave Casper

d. Offensive tackle Wes Shivers

12. After engaging in two memorable fights with his former Tennessee teammates as a newly traded member of the New England Patriots, ex-Titan linebacker Akeem Ayers earned the nickname "The Vengeful Ex."

a. True

b. False

13. Which current Titan is known to teammates by the nickname "The Father of Nashville?"

a. Quarterback Ryan Tannehill

b. Running back Derrick Henry

c. Offensive tackle Taylor Lewan

d. Head coach Mike Vrabel

14. Most NFL fans knew Oiler coach "Bum" Phillips only by his nickname. What was Phillips' real first name?

a. Ferguson

b. Phillip

c. Oail

d. Wade

15. At times during his tenure in Houston, Oiler wide receiver Haywood Jeffires was referred to by all of the following nicknames except for which one?

a. "Wood"

b. "Freakwood"

c. "Driftwood"

d. "Charcoal"

16. Tennessee wide receiver Andre Johnson was called "Grandpa Dre" by his young teammates because he was brought in at age 35 to provide leadership and playoff experience while demonstrating how to act like a professional athlete.

a. True

b. False

17. Long-time Houston Oiler linebacker Robert Brazile shared a nickname with which famous comic book villain?

a. "Dr. Doom"

b. "The Green Goblin"

c. "Thanos"

d. "The Joker"

18. What was the nickname that Titan running back Chris Johnson told reporters he decided to give himself at the beginning of the 2009 NFL season?

a. "The Unstoppable Force"

b. "Mr. End Zone"

c. "Every Coach's Dream"

d. "Run Fast, Get Paid"

19. Due to his powerful rushing style, Houston Oiler running back Charley Tolar was known by which of the following nicknames?

a. "The Human Bowling Ball"

b. "Rolling Thunder"

c. "Big Bag of Butcher Knives"

d. "Mack Truck"

20. Tennessee coach Jeff Fisher had such a long tenure with the franchise that he was eventually nicknamed "Mr. Titan."

a. True

b. False

QUIZ ANSWERS

1. C – St. Louis Rams

2. B – False

3. D – "The Eighth Wonder of the World"

4. C – Defensive end Jevon Kearse

5. B – In high school, he accepted a dare to dye his shoes differently from the black color worn by the rest of the team.

6. A – "The Steamroller"

7. A – True

8. C – "Crystal Chandelier"

9. B – Because he changed directions often, and on a dime, just like the popular video game character

10. D – "Air"

11. C – Tight end Dave Casper

12. B – False

13. C – Offensive tackle Taylor Lewan

14. C – Oail

15. B – "Freakwood"

16. B – False

17. A – "Dr. Doom"

18. C – "Every Coach's Dream"

19. A – "The Human Bowling Ball"

20. B – False

DID YOU KNOW?

1. Titan quarterback Ryan Fitzpatrick was noted for his streaky play and, depending on whether the streak was good or bad, he was known as "Fitzmagic" or "Fitztragic."

2. Fans of the Titans often attend games wearing helmets or hats with fake flames attached. The fans are known as "Flameheads" and they took their inspiration from a Titan in Greek mythology, Prometheus.

3. The University of Wisconsin-Oshkosh uses the nickname "Titans" and the franchise has actually drafted a player (guard Claire Rasmussen) from the school. However, he was drafted in 1970 when the team was still known as the Houston Oilers, which means that every player selected by the Tennessee Titans has had to change his team nickname upon joining the NFL.

4. When the Titans featured the speedy Chris Johnson and the bruising LenDale White at running back, they could not use the common nickname "Thunder and Lightning" because White had been known that way during his college career at USC where he partnered with the elusive Reggie Bush. White and Johnson, therefore, became known instead as "Smash and Dash" in Tennessee.

5. The Houston Astrodome had several nicknames but was called "the House of Pain" specifically when the Oilers were playing there in the 1980s.

6. After a 2009 performance in which he rushed for over 2,000 yards and set the NFL record for most yards from scrimmage at 2,509, Tennessee running back Chris Johnson was given the nickname "CJ2K."

7. In 2000, the Titans were involved in a play so memorable that it was given its own nickname. Down one point in the playoffs to the Buffalo Bills with just 16 seconds left, tight end Frank Wychek grabbed the ball after the Bills kicked off and lateralled across the field to wide receiver Kevin Dyson who took off for a 75-yard game-winning touchdown. The play was dubbed "the Music City Miracle."

8. One other play that was heartbreaking for Tennessee fans would become known simply as "the Tackle." It also involved Kevin Dyson, who caught a pass on the final play of Super Bowl XXXIV with the Titans needing to go 10 yards to score a game-tying touchdown to send the contest to overtime. Dyson ran, dove, and stretched for the goal line while being wrapped up by St. Louis Rams linebacker Mike Jones, but came up just a few inches short as Tennessee was defeated.

9. When the Houston Oilers were racking up points during the 1980s with their run and shoot offense, opposing coach Buddy Ryan was frustrated with their scheme and referred to it unhappily as "Chuck and Duck."

10. Houston Oiler wide receivers Bill Groman and Charlie Hennigan were both deep threats who could score from anywhere on the field. Together, the duo was often referred to as "The Long Distance Twins."

CHAPTER 4:

THE QUARTERBACKS

QUIZ TIME!

1. Which of these Titan quarterbacks has been sacked by opponents the most times during the span of his career (315 times sacked)?

   a. Dan Pastorini
   b. Steve McNair
   c. Warren Moon
   d. Marcus Mariota

2. The legendary George Blanda holds the top-four spots on the Titans' all-time list of most passing touchdowns thrown in a season.

   a. True
   b. False

3. Which quarterback has thrown the most interceptions in Tennessee franchise history?

   a. Warren Moon
   b. Steve McNair

c. George Blanda

d. Dan Pastorini

4. Who is the franchise's all-time career leader in passing yards?

    a. Steve McNair

    b. George Blanda

    c. Dan Pastorini

    d. Warren Moon

5. Who set the franchise record for passing yards in a season by a Tennessee/Houston quarterback with 4,690 (the only one ever to crack 4,000)?

    a. Warren Moon

    b. Ryan Tannehill

    c. Steve McNair

    d. George Blanda

6. How many players who have played quarterback for the Titans have been elected to the Pro Football Hall of Fame?

    a. 1 player – George Blanda

    b. 2 players – George Blanda and Warren Moon

    c. 3 players – George Blanda, Warren Moon, and Ken Stabler

    d. 4 players – George Blanda, Warren Moon, Ken Stabler, and Steve McNair

7. Warren Moon played more games at QB for the Titans than any other player.

    a. True

    b. False

8. One journeyman Titan quarterback has been a member of nine NFL teams, more than any other franchise leader. Who was this well-traveled player?

    a. Chris Chandler

    b. Ryan Fitzpatrick

    c. Kerry Collins

    d. Matt Cassel

9. Which Titan was the youngest player in the team's history to start at quarterback at just 21 years old?

    a. Marcus Mariota

    b. Steve McNair

    c. Zach Mettenberger

    d. Jacky Lee

10. Which Houston quarterback took over from the great George Blanda and started the most games for the Oilers after Blanda moved to the Oakland Raiders to become primarily a kicker in 1967?

    a. Don Trull

    b. Charley Johnson

    c. Pete Beathard

    d. Dan Pastorini

11. How old was Titan legend George Blanda when he retired from his playing days in the NFL?

    a. 39 years old

    b. 43 years old

    c. 48 years old

    d. 50 years old

12. Titan QB Billy Volek named previous QB Steve McNair as the godfather when his daughter Susan was born in 2006.

   a. True
   b. False

13. The highest quarterback rating put up by a Houston Oiler/Tennessee Titan for a full season was 117.5. Which QB scored this franchise-high mark?

   a. Steve McNair
   b. Warren Moon
   c. Ryan Tannehill
   d. Dan Pastorini

14. Before joining the Houston Oilers in 1984, legendary quarterback Warren Moon set a Canadian Football League record that has not yet been matched by winning five consecutive Grey Cups with which Canadian franchise?

   a. Toronto Argonauts
   b. Edmonton Eskimos
   c. Calgary Stampeders
   d. Winnipeg Blue Bombers

15. Titan leader Steve McNair holds the franchise record for most rushing yards in a season by a quarterback, which he set in 1997. How many yards did he rack up?

   a. 674 yards rushing
   b. 719 yards rushing
   c. 855 yards rushing
   d. 926 yards rushing

16. Warren Moon won both a college national championship and a Super Bowl championship.

    a. True
    b. False

17. Which of the following Hall of Fame "firsts" is the only one that Oiler quarterback Warren Moon did not achieve during his career?

    a. First player elected to the Canadian Football Hall of Fame and the Pro Football Hall of Fame
    b. First African-American Pro Football Hall-of-Famer to play the quarterback position
    c. First Houston Oiler quarterback elected to the Pro Football Hall of Fame
    d. First undrafted quarterback to be elected to the Pro Football Hall of Fame

18. Which of the following is NOT a football fact about Houston Oiler quarterback Oliver Luck?

    a. He was the commissioner and CEO of the short-lived XFL before it filed for bankruptcy.
    b. He was the general manager for the Frankfurt Galaxy and Rhein Fire in NFL Europe.
    c. He is the father of highly acclaimed Indianapolis Colts quarterback Andrew Luck.
    d. He told Oiler coach Hugh Campbell that the team should sign CFL standout Warren Moon, who would make a better starter than Luck as the team's QB.

19. Which of the following is NOT a life fact about Houston Oiler quarterback Oliver Luck?

    a. He is a long-standing member of the American Council on Germany.

    b. He was an Academic All-American and a finalist for a Rhodes scholarship and graduated magna cum laude from West Virginia University.

    c. He ran for president in the 1992 election but lost in the Democratic primary to Arkansas governor Bill Clinton.

    d. He was the general manager of Major League Soccer's Houston Dynamo franchise.

20. Among quarterbacks who have started at least five games with Tennessee, Lynn Dickey has the highest interception percentage, with 9.5% of his passes thrown being picked off.

    a. True
    b. False

QUIZ ANSWERS

1. C – Warren Moon

2. B – False

3. C – George Blanda

4. D – Warren Moon

5. A – Warren Moon

6. C – 3 players – George Blanda, Warren Moon, and Ken Stabler

7. A – True

8. B – Ryan Fitzpatrick

9. D – Jacky Lee

10. C – Pete Beathard

11. C – 48 years old

12. B – False

13. C – Ryan Tannehill

14. B – Edmonton Eskimos

15. A – 674 yards rushing

16. B – False

17. C – First Houston Oiler quarterback elected to the Pro Football Hall of Fame

18. D – He told Oiler coach Hugh Campbell that the team should sign CFL standout Warren Moon, who would make a better starter than Luck as the team's QB.

19. C – He ran for president in the 1992 election, but lost in the Democratic primary to Arkansas governor Bill Clinton.

20. A - True

DID YOU KNOW?

1. Jacky Lee owns the longest passing play in Titan history. He found talented receiver Willard Dewveall for a 98-yard touchdown toss that helped the Houston Oilers defeat the San Diego Chargers in 1962.

2. Until 2019, no Titan quarterback had ever completed 70% of his passes in a season. Ryan Tannehill became the team's most accurate field general when he hit 70.3%.

3. Warren Moon could have used some better blocking when he became the Oiler QB in 1984. He was sacked a whopping 47 times, the highest total in team history. It did not get much better in 1985, as Moon was taken down 46 times that year for the second highest franchise total.

4. Four quarterbacks who've started for the team have played their entire NFL careers with Tennessee. Cody Carlson played for seven seasons with the Oilers, Gifford Nielsen spent six seasons with the franchise, Oliver Luck stayed for five seasons, and Jake Locker stayed with the team for all of his four years.

5. Quarterback Steve McNair had the longest tenure as Titan QB. McNair played for the team for over a decade, from 1995 to 2005, until the team drafted Vince Young in 2006 and McNair moved to the Baltimore Ravens.

6. Warren Moon played for 17 years in the NFL, mostly with the Houston Oilers, but also in short stints with three

other franchises. During that time, Moon never won a Super Bowl ring but he did earn one eventually, as a broadcaster with the Seattle Seahawks in 2014.

7. In 2003, Titan quarterback Steve McNair won the NFL MVP award, becoming the first African-American passer ever to do so.

8. Houston Oiler quarterback Dan Pastorini loved life in the fast lane, both literally and figuratively. Aside from his time on the field, some of Pastorini's exploits included marrying a model, judging wet T-shirt contests, posing nude for *Playgirl* magazine, appearing in B-movies, and racing both hydroplanes and dragsters. Pastorini also wrote an autobiography called *Taking Flak: My Life in the Fast Lane*.

9. Early in his career, Warren Moon was the first professional quarterback to throw for 5,000 passing yards in a season, which he accomplished with the CFL's Edmonton Eskimos in both 1982 and 1983. After moving to the Houston Oilers in 1984, he immediately set their single-season franchise record for most passing yards, which was just 3,338 at the time.

10. Titan quarterback Ryan Tannehill is quite religious and includes "Colossians 3:23" when he gives fans autographs. This bible verse is a reference to working hard and willingly for God, which Tannehill draws much inspiration from.

CHAPTER 5:

THE PASS CATCHERS

QUIZ TIME!

1. Five wide receivers have recorded over 40 career touchdown catches for the Titans. Which one of them has the most?

   a. Charlie Hennigan
   b. Haywood Jeffires
   c. Derrick Mason
   d. Drew Hill

2. No one in Titan history is within 100 receptions of Ernest Givins at the top of Tennessee's record book.

   a. True
   b. False

3. Who is the franchise's single-season leader in receiving touchdowns scored with 17?

   a. Flanker Charlie Hennigan
   b. Wide receiver A.J. Brown
   c. Tight end Jonnu Smith
   d. Left end Bill Groman

4. Who holds the all-time career franchise record for receiving yardage for the Titans?

   a. Wide receiver Ken Burrough
   b. Tight end Frank Wychek
   c. Wide receiver Ernest Givins
   d. Tight end Delanie Walker

5. Which of the following academic degrees did Titan wide receiver Kevin Dyson NOT earn after his playing career ended?

   a. A master's degree in leadership
   b. A doctorate in communications
   c. A master's degree in teaching
   d. A doctorate in education leadership and practical practice

6. Only one Titan with at least 100 receptions has averaged 20 yards per catch over his career. Which athlete has shown this amazing big play ability?

   a. Wide receiver A.J. Brown
   b. Tight end Dave Casper
   c. Left end Bill Groman
   d. Wide receiver Kenny Britt

7. Before becoming a valuable member of the Houston Oilers, wide receiver Charlie Hennigan had been a high school biology teacher.

   a. True
   b. False

8. Which Titan pass-catcher has played more NFL games with the franchise than any other receiver?

    a. Wide receiver Ken Burrough
    b. Tight end Frank Wychek
    c. Wide receiver Ernest Givins
    d. Wide receiver Haywood Jeffires

9. Four pass catchers have at least 480 career receptions for the Tennessee Titans. Which of the following players is NOT in that club?

    a. Wide receiver Derrick Mason
    b. Wide receiver Haywood Jeffires
    c. Wide receiver Ernest Givins
    d. Tight end Frank Wychek

10. Despite all his accomplishments, Ernest Givins has more career fumbles than any other Titan wide receiver. How many times did he cough up the ball?

    a. 32 times
    b. 26 times
    c. 22 times
    d. 15 times

11. At the end of the 2020 NFL season, the Titans had a dozen wide receivers under contract for 2021. Which one of those wide receivers was signed for the highest base salary at just over $1 million?

    a. Josh Reynolds
    b. A.J. Brown

c. c. Marcus Johnson

d. Rashard Davis

12. Wide receiver Derrick Mason was the last active player in the NFL who had played for the Oilers before the franchise was officially renamed the Titans.

a. True

b. False

13. How many Titan tight ends have caught over 300 passes for the club during their careers?

a. One: Frank Wychek

b. Two: Frank Wychek and Delanie Walker

c. Three: Frank Wychek, Delanie Walker, and Bo Scaife

d. Five: Frank Wychek, Delanie Walker, Bo Scaife, Jared Cook, and Alvin Reed

14. Which two teammates posted the highest combined receiving yardage total in a season for the Titans, totaling 2,921 yards?

a. Wide receivers Charlie Hennigan and Bill Groman in 1961

b. Wide receivers Drew Hill and Tim Smith in 1985

c. Wide receivers Derrick Mason and Drew Bennett in 2003

d. Wide receivers A.J. Brown and Corey Davis in 2019

15. The Houston Oilers were so successful in the AFL that they were able to sign wide receiver Willard Dewveall, who would catch the longest touchdown pass in franchise history, away from which NFL franchise?

a. Green Bay Packers

b. Minnesota Vikings

c. Cleveland Browns

d. Chicago Bears

16. Titan wide receiver Nate Washington is the NFL's all-time leader in receiving yards by an undrafted player.

a. True

b. False

17. Houston Oiler legend Billy "White Shoes" Johnson went on to play wide receiver with the Montreal Alouettes in the Canadian Football League, on the same team as which famous professional wrestler?

a. Darren "Droz" Drozdoff

b. Bret "The Hitman" Hart

c. Lex "The Total Package" Luger

d. Dwayne "The Rock" Johnson

18. Which Titan recorded the most catches in one season for the team with 101 passes?

a. Wide receiver Derrick Mason in 2003

b. Tight end Delanie Walker in 2015

c. Wide receiver Haywood Jeffires in 1991

d. Wide receiver Charlie Hennigan in 1964

19. Which two teammates posted the highest touchdown reception total in a season for the Titans, converting 29 passes into scores?

a. Wide receivers Haywood Jeffires and Ernest Givins in 1992

b. Tight end Jonnu Smith and wide receiver A.J. Brown in 2020

c. Wide receivers Charlie Hennigan and Bill Groman in 1961

d. Tight end Delanie Walker and wide receiver Kenny Britt in 2012

20. Over the years, Titan tight end Frank Wychek threw 6 passes on trick plays and finished his career with 2 passing touchdowns and a perfect passer rating of 158.3.

a. True

b. False

QUIZ ANSWERS

1. A – Charlie Hennigan

2. B – False

3. D – Left end Bill Groman

4. C – Wide receiver Ernest Givins

5. B – A doctorate in communications

6. C – Left end Bill Groman

7. A – True

8. A – Wide receiver Ken Burrough

9. A – Wide receiver Derrick Mason

10. D – 15 times

11. B – A.J. Brown

12. A – True

13. B – Two TEs: Frank Wychek and Delanie Walker

14. A – Wide receivers Charlie Hennigan and Bill Groman in 1961

15. D – Chicago Bears

16. B – False

17. C – Lex "The Total Package" Luger

18. D – Wide receiver Charlie Hennigan in 1964

19. C – Wide receivers Charlie Hennigan and Bill Groman in 1961

20. A – True

DID YOU KNOW?

1. Titan icon Derrick Mason ranks 27th on the all-time list for most receiving yards in the NFL with 12,061. He is just behind Pittsburgh Steeler wideout Hines Ward and just ahead of Hall-of-Fame Dallas Cowboy wide receiver Michael Irvin.

2. The single-game record for most receptions in franchise history is held by three players. Charlie Hennigan reeled in 13 passes in a game in 1961 to set the mark and it has since been equaled by Haywood Jeffires and Drew Bennett.

3. Only 17 tight ends in NFL history have recorded more than 500 pass receptions. The Titans boast two of them: Frank Wychek, who had 505 catches, and Delanie Walker, who had 504.

4. For a few years in the early 2000s, Tennessee had both wide receiver Kevin Dyson and his brother, cornerback Andre Dyson, in their lineup. The Dysons became the first brothers in the history of the league to both score a touchdown in the same game for the same team.

5. Sixty years have passed since Houston Oiler wide receiver Bill Groman's rookie season, yet he still holds the record for most receiving yards by a rookie. In 1960, Groman racked up 1,473 yards through the air. The closest anyone has come to matching that was in 2020 when Justin

Jefferson of the Minnesota Vikings fell just shy at 1,400 yards.

6. No Titan has ever scored more than 3 receiving touchdowns in a single game. Many Oilers and Titans have reached three scores, but the most notable was probably when wide receiver Drew Bennett did it in back-to-back weeks in 2004.

7. Oiler wide receiver Ernest Givins had many opportunities to celebrate on the field, as he had 46 touchdowns with the franchise. Givins relished these opportunities and frequently broke out into "the Electric Slide," a dance move popularized by Jamaican singers Marcia Griffiths and Bunny Wailer.

8. Superstar Oiler receiver Charlie Hennigan had a day (January 19) declared "Charlie Hennigan Day" in his honor in his hometown of Minden, Louisiana. Ironically, the original day was scheduled for a week earlier but had to be delayed due to weather concerns.

9. The pronunciation of Houston Oiler wide receiver Haywood Jeffires' last name was often mangled, as it is pronounced like the more commonly seen "Jeffries." In Tecmo Super Bowl, a classic video game produced by Nintendo, his name was spelled incorrectly as "Jeffries" due to that pronunciation.

10. Houston Oiler legend Billy "White Shoes" Johnson was among the first players in the NFL to celebrate touchdowns elaborately. Johnson did a popular dance known as the

"Funky Chicken" as early as 1974 and his profile soared as fans had no trouble distinguishing him from other players.

CHAPTER 6:

RUNNING WILD

QUIZ TIME!

1. Who holds the Titan single-season franchise rushing yardage record with 2,027 yards?

   a. Chris Johnson
   b. Derrick Henry
   c. Earl Campbell
   d. Eddie George

2. It is a Titan tradition for every running back to tap his helmet against the helmets of the starting offensive linemen following the warmup before a game.

   a. True
   b. False

3. Which running back accumulated the most carries (46) for Tennessee without scoring a rushing touchdown?

   a. Quarterback Chris Chandler
   b. Running back Dion Lewis
   c. Kick returner Dexter McCluster
   d. Running back Ward Walsh

4. Which of the following is NOT an actual quote by an opposing player about Houston Oiler running back Earl Campbell?

    a. "When you finished a game against Earl, you had to sit in a tub with Epsom salts."
    b. "Earl Campbell was put on this earth to play football."
    c. "Every time you hit him, you lower your own IQ."
    d. "They call his style 'bruising,' but it's more like 'bone-crunching.'"

5. How many running backs have carried the ball at least 1,000 times for the Titans?

    a. 2
    b. 3
    c. 5
    d. 7

6. No Titan running back with at least 20 games played has averaged over 100 yards per game during his career. The legendary Earl Campbell is the closest; what is his average?

    a. 88.5 yards per game
    b. 94.2 yards per game
    c. 96.1 yards per game
    d. 99.3 yards per game

7. Earl Campbell had 73 rushing touchdowns with the Titans, which is more than the next two highest Tennessee running backs combined.

a. True

b. False

8. In which season did RB Chris Johnson record an astonishing 5.6 yards per carry for Tennessee?

a. 2009

b. 2010

c. 2012

d. 2013

9. Which Tennessee running back (with at least 300 carries) has the highest career yards gained per attempt, at an even 5.0?

a. Hoyle Granger

b. Chris Johnson

c. Derrick Henry

d. Gary Brown

10. Derrick Henry recorded his first NFL touchdown against which NFL team?

a. Tampa Bay Buccaneers

b. Jacksonville Jaguars

c. Indianapolis Colts

d. New York Jets

11. How many of the Titans' top 10 seasons for rushing touchdowns were recorded by the great Earl Campbell?

a. 1

b. 2

c. 4

d. 8

12. Houston Oiler icon Earl Campbell won the NFL's Offensive Player of the Year Award in his first, second, and third years in the league.

   a. True
   b. False

13. Which Tennessee running back has the most career fumbles, with 39?

   a. Mike Rozier
   b. Eddie George
   c. Ronnie Coleman
   d. Earl Campbell

14. Which Titan had the highest single-season rushing yards per game, with an average of 128.9?

   a. Eddie George
   b. Chris Brown
   c. Earl Campbell
   d. Derrick Henry

15. Which of the following unusual careers was adopted by Houston Oiler running back Billy Cannon after he had retired from football?

   a. Marine biologist
   b. Taxidermy salesman
   c. Prison dentist
   d. Lighthouse keeper

16. When the Titans vanquished the Pittsburgh Steelers in a 2008 game, running back LenDale White endeared himself

to Tennessee fans and upset nearly everyone else by publicly trampling on one of Pittsburgh's popular "Terrible Towels" after the victory.

a. True
b. False

17. Titan running back Derrick Henry prominently features a tattoo of whose portrait across his chest?

a. Pro Football Hall-of-Fame running back Jim Brown
b. Rapper and entertainment mogul Jay Z
c. His grandmother Gladys
d. Jesus Christ

18. Which of the following is NOT a fact about enigmatic Titan running back Eddie George?

a. He earned his bachelor's degree in the field of landscape architecture.
b. He campaigned for the United States Senate as a Democrat in 2008 but lost the election.
c. In retirement, he starred in a Broadway musical production of "Chicago."
d. He is married to an entertainer who has appeared on the television show "Survivor" and sang in the group "Sisters With Voices."

19. Oiler running back Billy Cannon set a professional football record against the New York Titans in 1961 when he accumulated 373 all-purpose yards in a single game. Today, Cannon's mark is second all-time; how long did his record last?

a. Three weeks
b. Twelve years
c. Twenty-five years
d. Thirty-four years

20. As of 2020, the Titans have a decade-long streak of finishing the season with a 1,000-yard rusher, thanks to their identity as a grinding, run-first style offense.

a. True
b. False

QUIZ ANSWERS

1. B – Derrick Henry

2. B – False

3. D – Running back Ward Walsh

4. D – "They call his style 'bruising,' but it's more like 'bone-crunching.'"

5. C – 5

6. B – 94.2 yards per game

7. B – False

8. A –2009

9. C – Derrick Henry

10. B – Jacksonville Jaguars

11. C –4

12. A – True

13. D – Earl Campbell

14. C – Earl Campbell

15. C – Prison dentist

16. A – True

17. C – His grandmother Gladys

18. B – He campaigned for the United States Senate as a Democrat in 2008 but lost the election.

19. D – Thirty-four years

20. B – False

DID YOU KNOW?

1. Two running backs who have played for the Titans have been enshrined in the Pro Football Hall of Fame. Fullback John Henry Johnson got the call in 1987, and the most recent was Earl Campbell, who was elected in 1991.

2. Tennessee running back Chris Johnson was so explosive that he was a threat to score from anywhere on the field. Johnson holds the NFL record for most rushing touchdowns of 80 yards or more. Six times with the Titans, Johnson was able to break off one of those long scores, including a then-franchise record 94-yarder in 2012.

3. Eleven times in NFL history, a running back has scored 20 or more rushing touchdowns in a single season. Houston Oiler great Earl Campbell nearly added his name to the list in 1979 but was stopped just short with 19 rushing scores that year.

4. Titan running back Mike Rozier once appeared on the long-running television game show *Family Feud*, along with his wife, brother, and two sisters-in-law.

5. As if playing running back in the NFL was not dangerous enough to one's health, Houston Oiler running back Charley Tolar took it to another level. When not on the playing field, Tolar worked in the even more hazardous profession of fighting oil well fires.

6. After his playing career ended, former Oiler running back Alonzo Highsmith became a professional boxer. He was good at that, too. Fighting as a heavyweight, Highsmith finished his boxing career with a record of 27-1-2.

7. Titan franchise icon Eddie George was only the second running back in NFL history to reach 10,000 career yards rushing without ever missing a single game. The first was the man considered by many to be the best of all time, Jim Brown of the Cleveland Browns.

8. Running back Billy Cannon was so highly thought of that Houston Oiler owner Bud Adams signed him to the first football contract worth over $100,000…and also threw in a Cadillac for Cannon's dad.

9. Houston Oiler running back Earl Campbell was so revered in Texas that in 1981 the legislature made him an official State Hero. This was a rare honor, granted only to three people before Campbell: Sam Houston, Davy Crockett, and Stephen F. Austin.

10. Tennessee is the only NFL franchise that can boast two different running backs who have rushed for over 2,000 yards in a single season. Chris Johnson accomplished this for the Titans in 2009 and Derrick Henry also crossed that difficult threshold in 2020.

CHAPTER 7:

IN THE TRENCHES

QUIZ TIME!

1. Who was the last Titan defender to record the franchise high of 4 sacks in a game?

    a. Defensive tackle Ray Childress

    b. Linebacker Brian Orakpo

    c. Defensive end William Fuller

    d. Defensive end Jevon Kearse

2. The 2016 Tennessee Titans hold the NFL record for the heaviest combined weight of all starting offensive and defensive linemen.

    a. True

    b. False

3. Who is the Titans' all-time franchise leader in sacks, with 75.5?

    a. Defensive tackle Ray Childress

    b. Defensive end Jevon Kearse

    c. Defensive tackle Albert Haynesworth

    d. Defensive end Elvin Bethea

4. Which offensive lineman did the Titans select highest in the NFL draft, using a second overall draft choice?

   a. Tackle Greg Sampson in 1972
   b. Guard Chance Warmack in 2013
   c. Guard Mike Munchak in 1982
   d. Tackle Dean Steinkuhler in 1984

5. Which Titan offensive lineman has played the most games, with an astounding 296?

   a. Tackle Brad Hopkins
   b. Guard Mike Munchak
   c. Tackle Bruce Matthews
   d. Center Eugene Amano

6. Which Titan defensive lineman has played the most games?

   a. Defensive end Elvin Bethea
   b. Defensive tackle Jurrell Casey
   c. Defensive tackle Ray Childress
   d. Defensive tackle Henry Ford

7. After St. Louis offensive tackle Fred Miller shut down Titan pass rusher Jevon Kearse during Super Bowl XXXIV, the Titans signed him during the offseason.

   a. True
   b. False

8. Which Titan defender holds the team record with 22 career forced fumbles?

a. Linebacker Keith Bulluck

b. Defensive end Kyle Vanden Bosch

c. Defensive end Jevon Kearse

d. Defensive tackle Jurrell Casey

9. Three quarterbacks top the record books for most fumbles recovered for the Titans, but they tend to be cleaning up their own mess. Which defender created the most turnovers for Tennessee by scooping up opponents' fumbles?

a. Defensive end Elvin Bethea

b. Defensive tackle Glenn Montgomery

c. Linebacker John Grimsley

d. Defensive tackle Ray Childress

10. Defensive lineman Elvin Bethea played his entire NFL career with the Tennessee Titans after they drafted him in the third round in 1968. How long did that career last?

a. 13 seasons

b. 14 seasons

c. 16 seasons

d. 20 seasons

11. Oiler mainstay and NFL Hall-of-Fame guard Mike Munchak played over 150 NFL games with the club. Where does he rank in games played all-time for the franchise?

a. 2nd all-time

b. 8th all-time

c. Tied for 13th all-time

d. Tied for 20th all-time

12. Years before becoming a professional football player and standout offensive tackle with the Titans, Brad Hopkins was a basketball star who played on the same high school team as Boston Celtic first-round draft pick Acie Earl.

a. True

b. False

13. Which current Titan defensive lineman has the longest tenure in Tennessee?

a. Tackle Jeffrey Simmons

b. End Denico Autry

c. End Bud Dupree

d. Tackle Larell Murchison

14. Former Houston Oiler defensive end William Fuller is an active philanthropist who has done much charity work to help fund a cure for what disease that claimed his father's life?

a. Lung cancer

b. Alzheimer's disease

c. Lupus

d. Diabetes

15. In 2018, Titan offensive tackle Taylor Lewan signed a new contract for more money than any NFL offensive lineman ever had. As of the start of the 2021 NFL season, where does Lewan rank among compensation for linemen?

a. 1st overall
b. Tied for 4th overall
c. 8th overall
d. Tied for 13th overall

16. Titan legend Bruce Matthews played so long that he faced the Baltimore Colts in 1983 and the Baltimore Ravens in 1997 when both teams took the field for the final time at Baltimore's Memorial Stadium.

a. True
b. False

17. Houston Oiler defensive tackle Curley Culp had been a heavyweight wrestling champion in the NCAA and his strength elicited much praise, including all of these quotes except for which one?

a. "Every center in the league should have to go against Curley in order to know what it's like to go against the very best." – Kansas City Chiefs center Jack Rudnay
b. "One word comes to mind whenever I think about facing Curley: help." – Minnesota Vikings center Mick Tinglehoff
c. "Curley made (my 3-4 defense) work. He made me look smart." – Oiler coach Bum Phillips
d. "Curley Culp was perhaps the strongest man I ever lined up against." – Oakland Raiders center Jim Otto

18. Which two Titans were teammates on the offensive line for the team on the field and then worked together again on the team's coaching staff off the field?

    a. Brad Hopkins and Michael Roos
    b. Bob Talamini and Walt Suggs
    c. Benji Olson and David Stewart
    d. Bruce Matthews and Mike Munchak

19. Which of the following positions was NOT held by Oiler/Titan legend Mike Munchak between his stint as a guard with the team from 1982 to 1993 and his stint as the team's head coach from 2011 to 2013?

    a. Offensive quality control
    b. Offensive assistant
    c. Offensive advance scout
    d. Offensive line coach

20. Titan defensive tackle DaQuan Jones is a self-described "adrenaline junkie" who requested (and received) a clause in his contract allowing him to participate in activities such as bungee jumping, skydiving, and motorcycle racing. Jones was forced to stipulate that the Titans would not be liable to pay him if he suffered an injury during any of those activities.

    a. True
    b. False.

QUIZ ANSWERS

1. C – Defensive end William Fuller

2. B – False

3. D – Defensive end Elvin Bethea

4. D – Tackle Dean Steinkuhler in 1984

5. C – Tackle Bruce Matthews

6. A – Defensive end Elvin Bethea

7. A – True

8. C – Defensive end Jevon Kearse

9. D – Defensive tackle Ray Childress

10. C – 16 seasons

11. B – 8th all-time

12. A – True

13. A – Tackle Jeffrey Simmons

14. D – Diabetes

15. C – 8th overall

16. A – True

17. B – "One word comes to mind whenever I think about facing Curley: help." – Minnesota Vikings center Mick Tinglehoff

18. D – Bruce Matthews and Mike Munchak

19. C – Offensive advance scout

20. B – False

DID YOU KNOW?

1. Two defensive ends share the Tennessee record for most safeties created. Elvin Bethea and Jim Young both recorded two, while nobody else in franchise history has more than one.

2. The Matthews family spawned an NFL dynasty that benefitted the Titan franchise more than once. Primarily, it gave them Hall-of-Fame Titan offensive lineman Bruce Matthews, but the family also included Bruce's father Clay Sr., a tackle for the San Francisco 49ers; Bruce's brother Clay Jr., a linebacker for the Cleveland Browns; Bruce's nephews, Clay III of the Green Bay Packers and Casey of the Philadelphia Eagles; and Bruce's sons Jake, a tackle for the Atlanta Falcons, and Kevin, a center who also played for Tennessee.

3. Oiler defensive end John Matuszak was a star on the field who later became a star on the screen. In his retirement, Matuszak took up acting and appeared on popular television shows such as *M*A*S*H*, *The Dukes of Hazzard*, *The A-Team*, and *Miami Vice*. He is likely best known for his role of "Sloth" in the hit movie *The Goonies*.

4. Titan defensive tackle Albert Haynesworth played with a violent streak that occasionally crossed the line. In one incident, Haynesworth used his cleat to stomp on Dallas Cowboys center Andre Gurode's head. Because Gurode's

helmet was off, this opened a massive cut requiring 30 stitches to close. Haynesworth was handed a lengthy suspension and ordered to undergo anger management counseling.

5. DT Ray Childress once recovered 3 fumbles in a single game. It happened against the Washington Redskins in 1988 and helped Childress reach a total of 7 fumble recoveries on the season, which was just 2 short of the NFL record.

6. Offensive lineman Bruce Matthews was uncannily reliable for the Oilers and Titans. Matthews started nearly 300 NFL games, which not only leads the franchise but is the third most league-wide all-time, behind only superstar quarterbacks Tom Brady and Brett Favre.

7. Bruce Matthews was not only reliable but also versatile. Matthews started at least 16 games at left tackle, left guard, center, right guard, and right tackle, sliding along the line wherever Tennessee needed to plug a hole. He was also on the team's kicking unit, snapping to the punter and to the holder on field goals and point-after attempts.

8. Titan defensive tackle Jurrell Casey and linebacker Wesley Woodyard took up coaching in an unusual fashion. The duo created and coached a flag football team featuring the wives and girlfriends of Tennessee players.

9. Houston Oiler all-time team member Don Floyd was such a good defensive end that his high school in Midlothian, Texas, named a stadium after him. Curiously, they built a new stadium almost immediately and relegated Floyd's

namesake to a practice field, which upset many citizens. This led to the road to the new stadium being named after Floyd as well.

10. Defensive tackle Ray Childress is the all-time leading tackler for the franchise. Childress played in Houston with the Oilers for 11 seasons and racked up 858 tackles during that time.

CHAPTER 8:

THE BACK SEVEN

QUIZ TIME!

1. Which Titan defensive back is the franchise's all-time leader in interceptions with 45?

    a. Cornerback Cris Dishman

    b. Safety Jim Norton

    c. Cornerback W.K. Hicks

    d. Safety Fred Glick

2. During the 2010s poker craze, members of Tennessee's secondary and linebacking corps held a weekly game where, rather than playing for money, the losers had to tweet embarrassing things about themselves or flattering things about the winners.

    a. True

    b. False

3. Who holds the franchise record for most interceptions returned for a touchdown, with 9?

    a. Cornerback Miller Farr

    b. Cornerback Cortland Finnegan

c. Cornerback Vincent Fuller

d. Safety Ken Houston

4. Although sacks are usually not a high priority for defensive backs in most coaching systems, one Titan DB excelled at this skill, putting up 17 sacks in his career. Who?

a. Safety Keith Bostic

b. Cornerback Samari Rolle

c. Safety Blaine Bishop

d. Cornerback Logan Ryan

5. The initials in popular Oiler defensive back W.K. Hicks' name stand for what?

a. William Kenneth

b. Warren Kennedy

c. Wayne Kennard

d. Wilmer Kenzie

6. The most recent player to lead the Titans in tackles had 111 combined tackles in 2020. Who is it?

a. Linebacker Rashaan Evans

b. Cornerback Malcolm Butler

c. Linebacker Jayon Brown

d. Safety Kevin Byard

7. Titan linebacker Brian Orakpo was so well-respected that he was elected as a team captain in 2015, despite being a new free agent signing from the Washington Football Team and having no tenure in Tennessee.

a. True

b. False

8. Which of the following is NOT a fact about quirky Titan linebacker Derrick Morgan?

   a. Morgan follows a completely vegan diet and does promotions for the Beyond Meat company.

   b. Morgan created his own podcast, "Smash Hits," to discuss his favorite movies, songs, and television shows.

   c. Morgan once spent part of his offseason delivering hearing aids on a trip to many African countries.

   d. Morgan chose a cannabis theme for his cleats during a game against the Houston Texans.

9. Oiler linebacker Gregg Bingham quite seriously took up which hobby when he was not playing football?

   a. Creating ships in bottles

   b. Building model trains

   c. Climbing mountains

   d. Collecting rare coins

10. In retirement, former Titan safety Blaine Bishop teams up with former Tennessee wide receiver Kevin Dyson to do the announcing for which of the following events?

    a. The championship game for Tennessee high school football

    b. The annual NCAA track and field championships

    c. The World Series of Poker in Las Vegas, Nevada

    d. The Daytona 500 NASCAR race

11. Oiler mainstay Gregg Bingham played over 170 NFL games with the club. Where does this linebacker rank in games played all-time for the franchise?

    a. Tied for 3rd
    b. 6th
    c. Tied for 9th
    d. 11th

12. Years after his playing and coaching careers were both over, Houston Oiler linebacker and Pro Football Hall-of-Famer Robert Brazile became a special needs teacher at a middle school in his hometown, Mobile, Alabama.

    a. True
    b. False

13. Which of the following positions did Hall-of-Fame Oiler safety Ken Houston NOT hold after retiring from his playing career?

    a. Head coach of the Wheatley High School football team in Houston, Texas
    b. Guidance counselor with the Houston Independent School District
    c. Defensive backs coach for the University of Houston Cougars football team
    d. Principal of Westbury High School in Houston, Texas

14. Which of these current Titan back seven players has been with the team for five seasons, the longest current tenure in Tennessee's back seven?

a. Safety Kevin Byard

b. Linebacker Jayon Brown

c. Safety Dane Cruikshank

d. Linebacker Harold Landry III

15. Which of the following statements about Titan cornerback Samari Rolle is NOT true:

a. His family background is Cuban and Bahamian.

b. He has three family members, Antrel, Myron, and Brian, who have all played on defense in the NFL.

c. He once lost a tooth during a game against the Detroit Lions and found it afterward, embedded in the bar of his facemask.

d. He was once on an airplane during a South African Safari with a few other NFL players and their wives when the door of the plane blew off mid-flight.

16. In 1977, cornerback Zeke Moore established the "Original Oiler" tradition, wherein he donated his gold pocket watch upon retirement to the next most experienced cornerback to take up the mantle for Houston. To this day, the watch hangs in cornerback Greg Mabin's locker and he must pass it on if he retires, is traded, cut, or signs elsewhere.

a. True

b. False

17. Since the NFL has kept track of solo tackles, which Tennessee defender has recorded the most in a single season, with 121?

a. Linebacker Stephen Tulloch

b. Safety Kevin Byard

c. Linebacker Keith Bulluck

d. Linebacker Randall Godfrey

18. Former Titan free safety Michael Griffin was noted for always wearing which of the following unusual items at team practices?

a. A pair of sunglasses

b. A surgical mask

c. A wristwatch

d. A set of ankle weights

19. In the 1991 NFL season, Oiler cornerback Cris Dishman had an incredible stretch of seven straight games in which he forced a turnover. Dishman bookended the streak, starting and completing it against the same team. Which team was it?

a. Cleveland Browns

b. Pittsburgh Steelers

c. Indianapolis Colts

d. Cincinnati Bengals

20. The Houston Oilers once started a linebacker named Ted Washington, whose son, also named Ted Washington, became a four-time Pro Bowler and Super Bowl champion in the NFL.

a. True

b. False

QUIZ ANSWERS

1. B – Safety Jim Norton

2. B – False

3. D – Safety Ken Houston

4. A – Safety Keith Bostic

5. D – Wilmer Kenzie

6. D – Safety Kevin Byard

7. A – True

8. B – Morgan created his own podcast, "Smash Hits," to discuss his favorite movies, songs, and television shows.

9. D – Collecting rare coins

10. A – The championship game for Tennessee high school football

11. B – 6th

12. A – True

13. D – Principal of Westbury High School in Houston, Texas

14. A – Safety Kevin Byard

15. C – He once lost a tooth during a game against the Detroit Lions and found it afterward, embedded in the bar of his facemask.

16. B – False

17. A – Linebacker Stephen Tulloch

18. C – A wristwatch

19. D – Cincinnati Bengals

20. A – True

DID YOU KNOW?

1. Passes defended is a stat that the NFL began using at the turn of the century. Cornerback Samari Rolle has long been the statistical record-holder for the Titans, having notched 79 by the time he left the team in 2004. No current Titan has more than 35 for the club.

2. Two members of the Titans' back seven, linebacker Brian Orakpo and free safety Michael Griffin, made the interesting decision to open a bakery devoted exclusively to cupcakes. Their shop, Gigi's Cupcakes, is located in Griffin's hometown of Austin, Texas.

3. Within a single position group, it is difficult to have a more diverse coaching background than former Titan cornerback Cris Dishman. Dishman has experience coaching defensive backs in the NFL, CFL, XFL, NCAA, and at IMG Academy (a boarding school in Florida that prepares student-athletes for professional careers).

4. In 1986, Houston Oiler safety Keith Bostic went to extremes to win a $20 bet with his teammate, cornerback Steve Brown. The two were known for their chatter on the field, so in order to settle who could keep quiet the longest, Bostic played during training camp with a piece of tape covering his mouth.

5. Titan cornerback Jason McCourty has a twin brother, Devin, who plays safety with the New England Patriots.

The two played in the same defensive backfield at Rutgers University and are one of just 13 sets of twins who have made it to the NFL.

6. Titan safety Michael Griffin always admired the ability of NFL quarterback Michael Vick. The two never got to be teammates in the NFL, but joined up together to play for a flag football team called the Roadrunners in the AFFL.

7. One defensive back and one linebacker who played for the Titan franchise have been enshrined in the Pro Football Hall of Fame. Safety Ken Houston was the first to be elected, in 1986, and linebacker Robert Brazile was elected in 2018.

8. Marcus Robertson brought his experience as a free safety for the Titans into his next position with the club: director of player development. Robertson's innovative techniques and dedication to player success won him and his assistants the Winston and Shell Award in 2006.

9. At the end of their careers, many players are cut or simply not given a new contract by their team. After linebacker Keith Bulluck retired from the Titans in 2012, head coach Mike Munchak said of him, "He played play in and play out as good as anyone in football during his 10 years with us here at the Titans."

10. Houston Oiler safety Ken Houston set an NFL record for most non-offensive touchdowns in a season that stood for 35 years. Houston scored 5 touchdowns in 1971, 4 on interception returns and 1 on a fumble return. The mark

was not passed until 2006 when Devin Hester managed six scores.

CHAPTER 9:

WHERE'D THEY COME FROM?

QUIZ TIME!

1. Where was legendary Titan quarterback Steve McNair born?

   a. Albany, New York
   b. Houston, Texas
   c. Mount Olive, Mississippi
   d. Baton Rouge, Louisiana

2. Oiler wide receiver Ernest Givins, who played nine years with the team, was born and raised in Houston, Texas.

   a. True
   b. False

3. In the 1961 draft, the Oilers chose multiple players from a few colleges. From which of the following schools did they only select one?

   a. Mississippi
   b. Mississippi State
   c. Colorado State
   d. Bowling Green

4. Which Titan running back earned the nickname "the Tyler Rose" because he was born in the city of Tyler, Texas?

    a. Derrick Henry
    b. Eddie George
    c. Earl Campbell
    d. Chris Johnson

5. From which team did the Titans acquire useful running back DeMarco Murray in a 2016 swap?

    a. Miami Dolphins
    b. Jacksonville Jaguars
    c. Dallas Cowboys
    d. Philadelphia Eagles

6. Which of the following is NOT an actual college program that Houston drafted a player from during the 1968 NFL draft?

    a. North Carolina A&T
    b. North Carolina Central
    c. La Verne
    d. North Carolina Tech

7. The Titans have drafted more players from the Michigan State Spartans than from the Michigan Wolverines.

    a. True
    b. False

8. Which three-time AFL Champion player released by the Houston Oilers went on to become a Super Bowl champion with Joe Namath's New York Jets?

a. Running back Sid Blanks

b. Guard Bob Talamini

c. Kicker George Blanda

d. Defensive end Don Floyd

9. One of the Titans' best trades saw them acquire quarterback Ryan Tannehill and a sixth-round pick in exchange for just fourth- and seventh-round picks. Which team regretted making that deal with Tennessee?

a. Miami Dolphins

b. Seattle Seahawks

c. Arizona Cardinals

d. Detroit Lions

10. In which West Coast city was Oiler franchise quarterback Warren Moon born in 1956?

a. San Diego, California

b. Vancouver, British Columbia

c. Seattle, Washington

d. Los Angeles, California

11. In their entire franchise history, the Titans have drafted only two players from Rutgers University in a non-expansion draft, and they took both in the same year. Which two players were they?

a. Running back Chris Johnson and defensive tackle Jurrell Casey

b. Wide receiver Charlie Hennigan and defensive end Elvin Bethea

c. Wide receiver Kenny Britt and defensive back Jason McCourty

d. Tight end Delanie Walker and wide receiver Kevin Dyson

12. Tennessee has never completed a trade with the Atlanta Falcons.

    a. True
    b. False

13. In 1978, the Titans traded tight end Jimmie Giles and first-, second-, third-, and fifth-round picks to the Tampa Bay Buccaneers for the rights to the top overall pick, so they could draft who?

    a. Running back Earl Campbell
    b. Offensive tackle Morris Towns
    c. Linebacker Robert Brazile
    d. Guard Mike Munchak

14. In 1964, the Titans drafted wide receiver Charley Taylor, who played for Arizona State University, in the second round. What was his college team's nickname?

    a. Aztecs
    b. Red Coyotes
    c. Cacti
    d. Sun Devils

15. Jevon Kearse played his college football as the defensive end at what college before coming to the Titans?

    a. Nebraska Cornhuskers
    b. Florida Gators

c. Oklahoma Sooners

d. Georgia Bulldogs

16. The Titans have never traded away a player who was born in the state of Tennessee.

a. True

b. False

17. Which college program did Estonian offensive tackle Michael Roos attend before his entrance into the NFL in 2005?

a. University of Connecticut

b. Florida International University

c. North Dakota State University

d. Eastern Washington University

18. Who/what did the Tennessee Titans trade to the Los Angeles Rams in 2016 in a deal that brought back the draft picks that led to the Titans selecting starting running back Derrick Henry, offensive tackle Jack Conklin, tight end Jonnu Smith, and wide receiver Corey Davis?

a. Tight end Delanie Walker and a second-round draft pick

b. Quarterback Marcus Mariota

c. The first overall pick in the NFL draft

d. Linebackers Derrick Morgan, Brian Orakpo, and a fourth-round draft pick

19. The talented and flamboyant Randy Moss was a member of which college squad before his time on the field with the Titans?

a. Marshall Thundering Herd

b. Oregon State Beavers

c. Virginia Tech Hokies

d. Penn State Nittany Lions

20. Tennessee has completed more trades with the Buffalo Bills than with any other NFL franchise.

a. True

b. False

QUIZ ANSWERS

1. C – Mount Olive, Mississippi

2. B – False

3. C – Colorado State

4. C – Earl Campbell

5. D – Philadelphia Eagles

6. D – North Carolina Tech

7. A – True

8. B – Guard Bob Talamini

9. A – Miami Dolphins

10. D – Los Angeles, California

11. C – Wide receiver Kenny Britt and defensive back Jason McCourty

12. B – False

13. A – Running back Earl Campbell

14. D – Sun Devils

15. B – Florida Gators

16. B – False

17. D – Eastern Washington University

18. C – The first overall pick in the NFL draft

19. A – Marshall Thundering Herd

20. B – False

DID YOU KNOW?

1. When the Titans needed to trade franchise quarterback Steve McNair away from Tennessee in 2006, the franchise sent him to the Baltimore Ravens to get a fourth-round draft pick instead of simply cutting him from the team.

2. Running back Billy Cannon was in high demand among NFL scouts. Cannon won the Heisman Trophy while playing at Louisiana State University and was chosen first overall by the Los Angeles Rams in the NFL draft. However, he chose to sign with the AFL's Houston Oilers instead and the team benefitted as Cannon helped lead them to two championships.

3. The Titans and Oakland/Los Angeles/Las Vegas Raiders have an interesting history of sharing quarterbacks. The signal-callers who have played for both squads include George Blanda, Dan Pastorini, Marcus Mariota, and Ken Stabler. All of these players went directly from one team to the other.

4. In 2005, Titan offensive lineman Michael Roos became the first NFL player who was a native of Estonia. Making that jump is still rare, as only defensive end Margus Hunt has joined Roos in that distinction in the years since.

5. One of the best free-agent signings made by the Titans occurred in 2006 when they inked center Kevin Mawae,

formerly of the New York Jets. Mawae made two Pro Bowls with Tennessee, helped running back Chris Johnson rush for over 2,000 yards, and enabled the Titans to equal their best win total for a season.

6. In a decision that was very popular at the time, Tennessee signed free agent defensive end Jadeveon Clowney in 2020. It was thought that Clowney would ignite the Titan pass rush but he got hurt and went on the injured reserve list a few months later and left the team without recording a single sack.

7. One of the most impactful trades ever made by the Titans was completed in 1980 with the Oakland Raiders. Houston sent starting quarterback Dan Pastorini to Oakland and received a new starting quarterback, Ken Stabler, in the blockbuster. Stabler outperformed Pastorini the following year and eventually made the Pro Football Hall of Fame but, when the Oilers and Raiders met in the playoffs, it was the Raiders who advanced with a win.

8. Fan favorite quarterback Dan Pastorini is the only player the Titans have ever selected who played in college for the Santa Clara University Broncos.

9. Defensive end Elvin Bethea remains the last North Carolina A&T player ever taken by the Titans in the NFL draft in 1968, despite his exemplary, Hall-of-Fame career.

10. The Houston Oilers hit the jackpot when they selected wide receiver Steve Largent 117th overall in 1976, as Largent became a Hall-of-Fame receiver. Unfortunately,

Houston didn't recognize this upside quite as much as it seemed because they traded Largent to the Seattle Seahawks for an eighth-round draft pick before he ever played a snap for the Oilers.

CHAPTER 10:

IN THE DRAFT ROOM

QUIZ TIME!

1. With their first-ever draft choice in 1961, the Houston Oilers selected which player who attended the University of Pittsburgh and would go on to make the Pro Football Hall of Fame?

    a. Linebacker Dave Wilcox
    b. Wide receiver Charley Taylor
    c. Tight end Mike Ditka
    d. Defensive back Ken Houston

2. For four consecutive years in the 1980s, the Oilers traded out of the first round of the NFL draft, acquiring more proven talent to compete with the Miami Dolphins.

    a. True
    b. False

3. From which of the following college football programs have the Titans drafted the most players?

    a. Texas Longhorns
    b. Texas Tech Red Riders

c. Texas A&M Aggies

d. Texas-El Paso Miners

4. During the first round of the 2020 NFL Draft, Tennessee congratulated which of the following players on becoming a Titan remotely, via webcam, because of the COVID-19 pandemic that prevented the usual handshakes on stage?

   a. Offensive tackle Isaiah Wilson of Georgia

   b. Cornerback Kristian Fulton of LSU

   c. Defensive tackle Jeffrey Simmons of Mississippi State

   d. The Titans did not own a first-round pick in the 2020 NFL Draft

5. The Titans selected two teammates from the Utah Utes back-to-back in the 2006 NFL Draft. Which teammates did they choose with the 245th and 246th picks?

   a. Linebacker Stephen Tulloch and defensive back Cortland Finnegan

   b. Wide receiver Joel Filani and offensive tackle Michael Otto

   c. Defensive ends Antwan Odom and Bo Schobel

   d. Linebacker Spencer Toone and running back Quinton Ganther

6. How many times in history has Tennessee used a top 10 overall draft pick?

   a. 11 times

   b. 19 times

   c. 28 times

   d. 34 times

7. The Titans have never held the first overall pick in the NFL draft in the entire history of the franchise.

    a. True
    b. False

8. In 2014, linebacker Avery Williamson was drafted by the Titans out of which school that is better known as a basketball powerhouse than a football school?

    a. Duke University
    b. University of Kansas
    c. Gonzaga University
    d. University of Kentucky

9. All-Pro defensive tackle Ray Childress was drafted by the Oilers third overall in the 1985 NFL Draft. Which Hall-of-Fame defensive lineman was selected ahead of him?

    a. Bruce Smith of the Buffalo Bills
    b. Reggie White of the Philadelphia Eagles
    c. Chris Doleman of the Minnesota Vikings
    d. Charles Haley of the San Francisco 49ers

10. Only one Ivy League player has ever been drafted by the Oilers or Titans in franchise history: defensive tackle David Howard. Which prestigious school did he attend?

    a. Brown University
    b. Harvard University
    c. Princeton University
    d. Yale University

11. How high did Tennessee select wide receiver Derrick Mason in the 1997 NFL Draft?

a. 1st round, 6th overall

b. 2nd round, 39th overall

c. 4th round, 98th overall

d. 7th round, 224th overall

12. Due in part to their long-standing rivalry with the Pittsburgh Steelers, the franchise has never drafted a player from the University of Pittsburgh.

a. True

b. False

13. Which Pro Football Hall-of-Famer did the Houston Oilers select with the first-round pick in the 1975 NFL draft that they acquired from the Kansas City Chiefs after trading defensive end John Matuszak away?

a. Defensive end Elvin Bethea

b. Quarterback Ken Stabler

c. Linebacker Robert Brazile

d. Running back Earl Campbell

14. Wide receiver Kenny Britt played four years of college ball for which program before becoming its first-ever first-round pick when he was drafted by the Titans 30th overall in 2009?

a. University of Nevada-Las Vegas

b. Rutgers University

c. Marshall University

d. University of New Mexico-Santa Fe

15. The Titans drafted two players from the Purdue Boilermakers who went on to play more than 170 NFL games each. Who were these players?

    a. Center Bobby Maples and defensive tackle Randy Starks
    b. Offensive tackle Jon Runyan and tight end Jimmie Giles
    c. Wide receiver Shawn Jefferson and punter Bobby Walden
    d. Linebacker Gregg Bingham and defensive back Cris Dishman

16. Quarterback Vince Young was such a talented athlete that he was drafted in not one but three sports (basketball, baseball, and football).

    a. True
    b. False

17. Which team did the Titans trade up with so they could select linebacker Rashaan Evans in the 22nd spot at the NFL draft in 2018?

    a. Minnesota Vikings
    b. Denver Broncos
    c. Baltimore Ravens
    d. Los Angeles Rams

18. In the 1982 NFL draft, Tennessee selected not one but two quarterbacks. Who did they take to attempt to lock down the position?

a. Oliver Luck and Ron Reeves

b. Craig Bradshaw and Gifford Nielsen

c. Steve Kincannon and Kelly Cochrane

d. Jim Everett and Warren Moon

19. Who did the Tennessee Titans select with their first-ever draft pick in 1999 after the franchise changed its name from Oilers to Titans?

a. Defensive tackle John Thornton

b. Wide receiver Kevin Dyson

c. Defensive end Jevon Kearse

d. Cornerback Samari Rolle

20. Between 1981 and 2012, Tennessee enjoyed a stretch in which they selected at least one player per year who lasted 100 games in the NFL.

a. True

b. False

QUIZ ANSWERS

1. C – Tight end Mike Ditka

2. B – False

3. A – Texas Longhorns

4. A – Offensive tackle Isaiah Wilson of Georgia

5. D – Linebacker Spencer Toone and running back Quinton Ganther

6. C – 28 times

7. B – False

8. D – University of Kentucky

9. A – Bruce Smith of the Buffalo Bills

10. A – Brown University

11. C – 4th round, 98th overall

12. B – False

13. C – Linebacker Robert Brazile

14. B – Rutgers University

15. D – Linebacker Gregg Bingham and defensive back Cris Dishman

16. B – False

17. C – Baltimore Ravens

18. A – Oliver Luck and Ron Reeves

19. C – Defensive end Jevon Kearse

20. A – True

DID YOU KNOW?

1. Some quarterbacks in the Titans' history have been talented enough to be drafted by Major League Baseball teams before choosing the NFL route. Steve McNair was chosen by the Seattle Mariners, Jake Locker was selected by the Los Angeles Angels, and Ken Stabler was drafted by the New York Yankees.

2. The most players Tennessee has drafted from any school is 20. This mark is currently held by the University of Texas and includes five first-rounders: quarterback Vince Young, running back Earl Campbell, defensive tackle Scott Appleton, linebacker Tommy Nobis, and defensive back Michael Griffin.

3. Tennessee has held the 77th and 159th overall picks nine times each, more than any other spots in the draft. When keeping those selections, their best draft picks from the 77th spot have been on the defensive line (Elvin Bethea and Jurrell Casey), while they have not had much success at 159th.

4. Tennessee has made two Michigan State Spartan players top-10 picks in the NFL draft. The team selected linebacker George Webster fifth overall in 1967 and offensive tackle Jack Conklin eighth overall in 2016.

5. The Titans have drafted 12 players from the University of Houston, 11 from the University of Tennessee, and 4 from

Tennessee State University. None of these local products have gone on to become Hall-of-Famers.

6. Tennessee has drafted precisely 13 players who have played just one game in the NFL, including at least one in every decade except the 1980s.

7. Of the draft spots in the top ten in the NFL draft, Tennessee has selected at third overall more than any other, choosing six players in that position. Four of those six times, the team has taken a quarterback: Dan Pastorini, Jim Everett, Steve McNair, and Vince Young.

8. The smallest draft class ever selected by the Titans in the NFL entry draft came in 2018 when they took only four players. The team grabbed linebackers Rashaan Evans and Harold Landry, cornerback Dane Cruikshank, and quarterback Luke Falk.

9. The largest Oiler draft class ever was selected in 1962, when the team drafted 34 players. Keeping all those names straight would have been difficult, as the team chose four Bills, three Bobs, a Bobby, and one Joe Bob.

10. The latest pick the Titans have made in the NFL draft was wide receiver Allen Misher from LSU, whom the team chose 479th overall in 1976. Misher never made it to the NFL. Center Hank Autry, the team's 430th overall pick from Southern Miss in 1969, was the latest pick they've made who actually

CHAPTER 11:

COACHES, GMS, & OWNERS

QUIZ TIME!

1. Who served as the Titans' first general manager?

   a. Sid Gillman

   b. Pop Ivey

   c. Bob Brodhead

   d. Don Suman

2. Tennessee general manager Floyd Reese once proposed a deal to the New England Patriots that would have sent Titan icon Steve McNair to Massachusetts in exchange for a young and then little-known Tom Brady.

   a. True

   b. False

3. The Titans' first head coach, Lou Rymkus, lasted for how long in that position with the franchise?

   a. Four games

   b. One season

   c. Two seasons

   d. Nine seasons

4. The Titans' most recent coach, Mike Vrabel, rose through the coaching ranks by starting as a position coach at which NCAA program before graduating to the NFL?

   a. Ohio State Buckeyes
   b. Florida State Seminoles
   c. Michigan State Spartans
   d. Colorado State Rams

5. Who has owned the Tennessee Titans for the longest amount of time?

   a. Susie Adams Smith
   b. Bud Adams
   c. Amy Adams Strunk
   d. Bob McNair

6. Of all the Tennessee bench bosses who have coached over 50 NFL games with the team, which one had the lowest winning percentage at only .493?

   a. Hugh Campbell
   b. Jack Pardee
   c. Mike Mularkey
   d. Wally Lemm

7. Tennessee is the only NFL franchise to have a player rise from competing on the field for the team to ownership of the team.

   a. True
   b. False

8. Which coach led the Titans to their first AFL championship?

a. Bum Phillips

b. Ed Biles

c. Lou Rymkus

d. Jerry Glanville

9. Which Tennessee general manager once played for the team?

a. Jon Robinson

b. Mike Reinfeldt

c. Floyd Reese

d. Ruston Webster

10. Who is the Tennessee leader with 141 regular-season coaching wins with the franchise?

a. Bum Phillips

b. Mike Vrabel

c. Jack Pardee

d. Jeff Fisher

11. The shortest term for a franchise ownership group was a stint of just two years in 2014-15. Who among the following people was not part of that ownership group?

a. Susie Adams Smith

b. Thomas Smith

c. Crystal Smith Jenkins

d. Amy Adams Hunt

12. Coach Jeff Fisher owns the Titan record for winning percentage, as he led the team to a .813 winning percentage in three different regular seasons.

a. True

b. False

13. How many Titan head coaches have spent their entire NFL coaching career with Tennessee?

    a. 2

    b. 4

    c. 6

    d. 8

14. Which two Titan general managers have led the franchise to the most playoff appearances, earning four apiece?

    a. Bum Phillips and Jon Robinson

    b. Sid Gillman and Mike Reinfeldt

    c. Mike Holovak and Floyd Reese

    d. Pop Ivey and Ladd Herzeg

15. Out of 17 seasons coaching the Titans, how many times did coach Jeff Fisher finish at .500 or better?

    a. 8 times

    b. 11 times

    c. 13 times

    d. 16 times

16. At one point in their history, the Titans employed four coaches over a decade who had all started for Tennessee at some point during their playing careers.

    a. True

    b. False

17. How did Amy Adams Strunk become the controlling owner of the Titans?

a. She purchased the team when the previous owners wished to sell.

b. She inherited the team from her father.

c. She forced a takeover of the corporation that had previously owned the team.

d. She was hired as CEO of the company that owned the team.

18. How many head coaches have roamed the sidelines for the Titans in their 60-year history?

    a. 9

    b. 13

    c. 19

    d. 25

19. How many Titan coaches have won an award as the NFL's top coach while behind the bench for Houston or Tennessee?

    a. None of them

    b. One of them: Jeff Fisher

    c. Two of them: Jeff Fisher and Bum Phillips

    d. Three of them: Jeff Fisher, Bum Phillips, and Jack Pardee

20. Titan owner Bud Adams once proposed trading franchises with New York Yankees owner George Steinbrenner, as part of a business deal.

    a. True

    b. False

QUIZ ANSWERS

1. D – Don Suman

2. B – False

3. C – Two seasons

4. A – Ohio State Buckeyes

5. B – Bud Adams

6. D – Wally Lemm

7. B – False

8. C – Lou Rymkus

9. B – Mike Reinfeldt

10. D – Jeff Fisher

11. C – Crystal Smith Jenkins

12. A – True

13. D –8

14. C – Mike Holovak and Floyd Reese

15. B – 11 times

16. B – False

17. B – She inherited the team from her father.

18. C – 19

19. A – None of them

20. B – False

DID YOU KNOW?

1. Six times in team history, the Titans fired a coach midway through a season. In 1961, this worked best: Lou Rymkus was fired after five games and Wally Lemm came aboard to lead the team to a 9-0 regular-season record and the AFL championship.

2. Three men have served as both coach and general manager of the Titans. Pop Ivey did both jobs in 1962 and 1963. Sid Gillman did it in 1973 and 1974. Bum Phillips lasted longer than Ivey and Gillman combined, holding down both positions from 1975 to 1980.

3. The first Houston Oiler coach, Lou Rymkus, was so pleased with his team's championship in the 1960 season that he had thousands of drinking glasses created to celebrate the occasion. The glasses were decorated not with a picture of a trophy, or the team's name, but with a picture of Rymkus' face.

4. The first Oiler general manager, Don Suman, was hired from a head coaching position in the college ranks. The twist? Suman was a college *basketball* coach at the time. Nonetheless, the hiring was a major success, as the Oilers won championships in both of Suman's two years at the helm.

5. Oiler coach Bum Phillips was known for his folksy charm and unique quotations. Some of the most popular

114

included: "The harder we played, the behinder we got"; (about Miami Dolphins great Don Shula) "He can take his'n and beat your'n and take your'n and beat his'n"; and (about Oiler QB Warren Moon) "That boy could throw a football through a car wash and not get it wet."

6. Head coach Jeff Fisher leads the Tennessee Titans in both regular-season wins (142) and losses (120). Fisher's win total is more than double the next highest coach, Bum Phillips, and his loss total is more than triple the next highest coach, Wally Lemm.

7. Setting the Titan franchise marks for wins and losses was not good enough for Jeff Fisher. After moving on from Tennessee to the St. Louis/Los Angeles Rams, Fisher racked up 45 more losses, giving him 165 regular-season defeats, which is the NFL's record for a head coach.

8. The Titans have never had a head coach who was born outside the United States. They have also never had a coach who was born in Tennessee, though the Oilers employed two head coaches from Texas, Sammy Baugh, and Bum Phillips.

9. Houston Oiler head coach Sammy Baugh still holds an NFL record from his days as a player. Though Baugh was better known as a passer, he had the highest punting average for a season, at 51.4 yards.

10. In league history, no franchise general manager has ever won the *Sporting News* NFL Executive of the Year Award.

CHAPTER 12:

ODDS & ENDS

QUIZ TIME!

1. Which Titan has won the most league MVP trophies while playing for Tennessee?

    a. Quarterback Warren Moon

    b. Running back Earl Campbell

    c. Quarterback Steve McNair

    d. Campbell and McNair are tied with one apiece.

2. The first Titan to win a major award given out by the NFL was franchise quarterback Dan Pastorini.

    a. True

    b. False

3. During which season did the Titans win their first Vince Lombardi Trophy as Super Bowl champions?

    a. The 1978 season

    b. The 1985 season

    c. The 2002 season

    d. The franchise has never won a Super Bowl.

4. In 2019, the NFL announced its all-time team, recognizing the 100 greatest players from the first 100 years of NFL history. How many of these players suited up for the Titans?

    a. 3 on offense, 1 on defense, and 1 on special teams
    b. 5 on offense, 3 on defense, and 2 on special teams
    c. 2 on offense, 4 on defense, and 1 on special teams
    d. 3 on offense, 3 on defense, and 0 on special teams

5. What negative event befell quarterback Ryan Tannehill before he returned to the field for the Titans and won the 2019 Comeback Player of the Year Award?

    a. He suffered a concussion the previous year and missed the remainder of the season.
    b. He broke his leg in a car accident driving home from practice during training camp.
    c. He was diagnosed with leukemia and had to undergo several grueling rounds of treatment.
    d. None of the above; he simply played very poorly the year before.

6. What is Mike Keith's connection to the Tennessee Titans?

    a. An architect who designed and built Nissan Stadium for the Titans
    b. A beloved groundskeeper who has worked for the Titans since their move from Houston
    c. A player agent who represented Steve McNair, Eddie George, and several others

d. A long-time radio announcer for the Titans on their home station

7. The Tennessee Titans have the most wins of any franchise in NFL history.

   a. True
   b. False

8. The Titan roster recently included quarterback Marcus Mariota and running back Derrick Henry, who won the Heisman Trophy in back-to-back years while playing with which college teams?

   a. The Washington Huskies and the Auburn Tigers
   b. The USC Trojans and the Miami Hurricanes
   c. The Oregon Ducks and the Alabama Crimson Tide
   d. The Ohio State Buckeyes and the Michigan Wolverines

9. How many Titan players have ever won the NFL's Defensive Player of the Year Award?

   a. 0
   b. 2
   c. 3
   d. 5

10. Only two players have spent an entire career of at least 15 years with the Titans/Oilers without ever starting a game for another NFL franchise. Who are these loyal athletes?

   a. Quarterback/kicker George Blanda and tight end Frank Wychek
   b. Safeties Ken Houston and Blaine Bishop

c. Defensive end Elvin Bethea and offensive lineman Bruce Matthews

d. Running back Eddie George and defensive tackle Jurrell Casey

11. Wide receiver Bill Groman was a key member of two championship teams in Houston, but he also won two more AFL championships with which other franchise?

   a. Kansas City Chiefs
   b. Denver Broncos
   c. New York Jets
   d. Buffalo Bills

12. Tennessee was the first NFL team to win the Super Bowl after losing the previous year.

   a. True
   b. False

13. Although their average yards per punt were in the mid-40s, Titan punters Jim Norton and Brett Kern share the Tennessee record for longest punt in franchise history with what distance?

   a. 68 yards
   b. 71 yards
   c. 79 yards
   d. 86 yards

14. Of the Oilers and Titans in the Pro Football Hall of Fame, only one player's career included time both in Houston and Tennessee. Which player?

a. Quarterback George Blanda

b. Offensive lineman Bruce Matthews

c. Quarterback Warren Moon

d. Guard Mike Munchak

15. Four Titans have been named the NFL's Offensive Player of the Year. Which of the following is the only one to receive that honor more than once?

a. Running back Earl Campbell

b. Quarterback Warren Moon

c. Running back Chris Johnson

d. Running back Derrick Henry

16. Long-time Oiler kicker Al Del Greco *missed* more field goals during his Titans career than any other Tennessee player has even *attempted*.

a. True

b. False

17. Which Titan kicker (with at least 50 kicks attempted), holds the team's highest field goal percentage, at 85.7% made?

a. Ryan Succop

b. Al Del Greco

c. Gary Anderson

d. Rob Bironas

18. Kicker Rob Bironas holds the franchise record for the longest field goal made, which was a last-minute game-winner against the Indianapolis Colts. How long was this record-setting kick?

a. 56 yards

b. 58 yards

c. 60 yards

d. 64 yards

19. Against which opposing team does the Titan franchise have the most playoff victories?

a. New England Patriots

b. Baltimore Ravens

c. Indianapolis Colts

d. Los Angeles Chargers

20. The Houston Oilers were the first professional football team to play its games in a domed stadium.

a. True

b. False

QUIZ ANSWERS

1. D – Campbell and McNair are tied with one apiece.

2. B – False

3. D – The franchise has never won a Super Bowl.

4. A – 3 on offense, 1 on defense, and 1 on special teams

5. D – None of the above; he simply played very poorly the year before.

6. D – A long-time radio announcer for the Titans on their home station

7. B – False

8. C – The Oregon Ducks and the Alabama Crimson Tide

9. A – 0

10. C – Defensive end Elvin Bethea and offensive lineman Bruce Matthews

11. D – Buffalo Bills

12. B – False

13. C – 79 yards

14. B – Offensive lineman Bruce Matthews

15. A – Running back Earl Campbell

16. B – False

17. D – Rob Bironas

18. C – 60 yards

19. D – Los Angeles Chargers

20. A – True

DID YOU KNOW?

1. Just one Titan has won the NFL's Walter Payton Man of the Year Award, quarterback Warren Moon in 1989.

2. Star defensive end Jared Allen missed the competition when he retired from the NFL in 2015, so Allen formed a competitive curling team featuring two former Tennessee Titans, offensive tackle Michael Roos and linebacker Keith Bulluck. The team aims to curl for the United States at the Winter Olympics.

3. The Titans count three franchise running backs who rank in the top 40 on the all-time list for most rushing yards in the NFL. Eddie George sits in the 28th spot, Chris Johnson 35th, and Earl Campbell 37th overall. All of them rank ahead of some notable Hall-of-Famers, such as Jim Taylor, Larry Csonka, and Terrell Davis.

4. During their time as the Houston Oilers, the franchise had a fight song that was very popular among fans. The song was called "Luv Ya Blue/Houston Oilers Number One," but its use was discontinued when the team moved to Tennessee.

5. The Titans' value is estimated at $2.3 billion by *Forbes* magazine, which ranks them as the 28th-most valuable NFL team, right between the Arizona Cardinals and Tampa Bay Buccaneers.

6. During their tenure in Houston, the team had an unofficial mascot known as "The Roughneck." Portrayed by fan Art Horridge, the mascot wore a team uniform complete with shoulder pads and a tin hat like those worn among oil field workers. He also carried a real steel wrench, just in case opposing fans gave him any trouble.

7. Tennessee has a winning record against 14 other current NFL teams. The Titans have got the better of Tampa Bay, Detroit, Buffalo, Jacksonville, Denver, New Orleans, Cincinnati, Chicago, Green Bay, Washington, Atlanta, Baltimore, the New York Jets, and the Houston Texans.

8. The franchise has played more games against the Cincinnati Bengals and Pittsburgh Steelers than any other teams in the NFL. The clubs have faced off 75 times apiece, with Tennessee holding a 40-34-1 record all-time against Cincinnati (good for a .540 winning percentage), and a 31-44 mark against Pittsburgh (.413).

9. The first touchdown pass and the first field goal in Titan history were completed by the same man. Houston Oiler legend and Pro Football Hall-of-Famer George Blanda notched both achievements in the Oilers' first game on September 11, 1960, against the Oakland Raiders.

10. The Houston Oilers were a part of the biggest comeback in NFL history, although unfortunately they were on the losing end. In a 1993 playoff game against the Buffalo Bills, Houston took a 32-point lead just after halftime, but eventually fell to the Bills 41-38 in overtime.

125

CONCLUSION

There you have it, an amazing collection of Titan trivia, information, and statistics at your fingertips! Regardless of how you fared on the quizzes, we hope that you found this book entertaining, enlightening, and educational.

Ideally, you knew many of these details but also learned a good deal more about the history of the Tennessee Titans, their players, coaches, management, and some of the quirky stories surrounding the team. If you got a little peek into the colorful details that make being a fan so much more enjoyable, then mission accomplished!

The good news is that the trivia doesn't have to stop there! Spread the word. Challenge your fellow Titan fans to see if they can do any better. Share some of the stories with the next generation to help them become Tennessee supporters too.

If you are a big enough Titan fan, consider creating your own quiz with some of the details you know that weren't presented here and then test your friends to see if they can match your knowledge.

The Tennessee Titans are a storied franchise. They have a long history with multiple periods of success (and a few that were less than successful). They've had glorious superstars, iconic moments, hilarious tales … but most of all they have wonderful, passionate fans. Thank you for being one of them.

Printed in the USA
CPSIA information can be obtained
at www.ICGtesting.com
LVHW010713171023
761330LV00005B/80